MW00442809

PRIMARY 1

Jacob's Ladder
READING
COMPREHENSION
PROGRAM
Grades K–1

PRIMARY

1

Jacob's Ladder

READING COMPREHENSION PROGRAM

Grades K–1

TAMRA STAMBAUGH, PH.D., &
JOYCE L. VANTASSEL-BASKA, ED.D.

PRUFROCK PRESS INC.
WACO, TEXAS

Copyright ©2012 Prufrock Press Inc.

Edited by Jennifer Robins

Production design by Raquel Trevino

ISBN-13: 978-1-59363-917-4

The purchase of this book entitles the buyer to reproduce student activity pages for single classroom use only. Other use requires written permission of publisher. All rights reserved.

At the time of this book's publication, all facts and figures cited are the most current available; all telephone numbers, addresses, and website URLs are accurate and active; all publications, organizations, websites, and other resources exist as described in this book; and all have been verified. The authors and Prufrock Press make no warranty or guarantee concerning the information and materials given out by organizations or content found at websites, and we are not responsible for any changes that occur after this book's publication. If you find an error or believe that a resource listed here is not as described, please contact Prufrock Press.

Prufrock Press Inc.
P.O. Box 8813
Waco, TX 76714-8813
Phone: (800) 998-2208
Fax: (800) 240-0333
http://www.prufrock.com

Contents

Part I:
Teachers' Guide
to *Jacob's Ladder Reading Comprehension Program*

Rationale

Constructing meaning of the written word is one of the earliest tasks required of students in schools. This skill occupies the central place in the curriculum at the elementary level. Yet, approaches to teaching reading comprehension often are "skill and drill," using worksheets on low-level reading material. As a result, students frequently are unable to transfer these skills from exercise pages and apply them to new, higher level reading material.

The time expended to ensure that students become autonomous and advanced readers would suggest the need for a methodology that deliberately moves students from simple to complex reading skills with grade-appropriate texts. Such a learning approach to reading skill development ensures that students can traverse easily from basic comprehension skills to higher level critical reading skills, while using the same reading stimulus to navigate this transition. Reading comprehension is enhanced by instructional scaffolding, moving students from lower order to higher order thinking, using strategies and processes to help students analyze passages (Villaume & Brabham, 2002). In addition, teachers who emphasize higher order thinking through questions and tasks (like those applied in this program) promote greater reading growth (Taylor, Pearson, Peterson, & Rodriguez, 2003).

Jacob's Ladder Primary 1 was written in response to teacher findings that students at the primary level who were already reading needed more rigorous materials and scaffolding to consistently work at higher levels of thinking in reading (VanTassel-Baska & Stambaugh, 2006a). This teacher insight is buttressed by findings from cognitive science that suggest that students need to have purpose and direction for discussions of text to yield meaningful learning and that scaffolding is a necessary part of enhancing critical reading behavior (Bransford, Brown, & Cocking, 2000). Similarly, Tivnan and Hemphill (2005) studied reading reform curricula in Title I schools and found that none of the reading programs emphasized skills beyond basic phonemic awareness, fluency, or limited comprehension. Therefore, supplementary curriculum that focuses on higher level thinking skills is needed.

The *Jacob's Ladder Reading Comprehension Program* is a compilation of the instructional scaffolding and reading exercises necessary to aid students in their journey toward becoming critical readers. Students learn concept development skills through generalizing, predicting and forecasting skills through delineating implications of events, and literary analysis skills through discerning textual meaning (VanTassel-Baska & Stambaugh, 2006a). The questions and tasks for each reading are open-ended, as this type of approach to responding to literature improves performance on comprehension tests (Guthrie, Schafer, & Huang, 2001). Progressing through the hierarchy of skills also requires students to reread the text, thereby improving metacomprehension accuracy (Rawson, Dunlosky, & Thiede, 2000).

Introduction to *Jacob's Ladder Primary 1*

Jacob's Ladder Primary 1 is a supplemental reading program that implements targeted readings from picture books, fables, and poetry that link reading comprehension and analysis with content disciplines. With this program, students engage in an inquiry process that moves from lower order to higher order thinking skills. Starting with basic literary understanding, students learn to critically analyze texts by determining implications and consequences, generalizations, main ideas, and/or creative synthesis. This book is suggested for gifted students in the primary grades (grades K–1) who are already reading or show advanced levels of understanding. It is used to enhance reading comprehension and critical thinking if stories are read aloud. Tasks are organized into six skill ladders, A–F, and each ladder focuses on a different skill. Students "climb" each ladder by answering lower level questions before moving to higher level questions (or rungs) at the top of each ladder. Each ladder stands alone and focuses on a separate critical thinking component in reading.

Ladder A focuses on implications and consequences. By leading students through sequencing and cause and effect activities, students learn to draw implications and consequences from readings. Ladder B focuses on making generalizations. Students first learn to provide details and examples and then move to classifying and organizing those details in order to make generalizations. Ladder C focuses on themes. Students begin by identifying the setting and characters and then make inferences about the literary situation. Ladder D focuses on creative synthesis by leading students through paraphrasing and summarizing activities. Ladder E focuses on students' emotional responses to the literature read by understanding emotion, expressing it, and then channeling it productively. Ladder F provides an emphasis on word play by engaging learners in understanding, applying, and embedding new vocabulary and literary devices in both their own and others' creative writing.

Table 1 provides a visual representation of the six ladders and corresponding objectives for each ladder and rung.

The *Jacob's Ladder* series consists of seven levels: Primary 1, Primary 2, and Levels 1–5. Levels 1–5 contain short stories, poetry, and nonfiction selections including biography, as well as at least two commensurate ladders for each selection, with the exception of Primary 1 poetry, which has one ladder per poem. *Jacob's Ladder Primary 1* and *Primary 2* differ from the rest of the series in that the majority of the short stories are Caldecott Medal or Caldecott Honor picture books. Many of the stories are intended to be read aloud for the first reading. In addition, although *Jacob's Ladder Primary 1* does contain poetry, it does not contain nonfiction selections.

Jacob's Ladder Primary 1 is recommended for gifted readers in grades K–1, *Jacob's Ladder Primary 2* is recommended for gifted readers in grades 1–2, *Jacob's Ladder Level 1* is recommended for bright students in grades 2–3, *Jacob's Ladder Level 2* is recommended for students in grades 4–5, and *Jacob's Ladder Level 3* is recommended for students in grades 5–6. *Jacob's Ladder Level 4* and *Level 5* are recommended for middle and early high school students in grades 7–9. However, teachers may find that they want to vary usage beyond the recommended levels, depending on student abilities. Evidence suggests that the curriculum can be successfully implemented with gifted learners and advanced readers, as well as promising learners, at different grade levels. Thus, the levels vary and overlap to provide opportunities for teachers to select the most appropriate set of readings for meaningful differentiation for their gifted, bright, or promising learners.

TABLE 1
Goals and Objectives of *Jacob's Ladder Primary 1* by Ladder and Rung

	Ladder A	Ladder B	Ladder C	Ladder D	Ladder E	Ladder F
Rung 3	**A3: Consequences and Implications** — Students will be able to predict character actions and story outcomes and make real-world forecasts.	**B3: Generalizations** — Students will be able to make general statements about a reading and/or an idea within the reading, using data to support their statements.	**C3: Theme/Concept** — Students will be able to identify a major idea or theme common throughout the text.	**D3: Creative Synthesis** — Students will create something new using what they have learned from the reading and their synopses.	**E3: Using Emotion** — Students will be able to analyze how emotion affects the passage and/or the reader.	**F3: Playing With Words** — Students will be able to accurately apply figurative language and new vocabulary to newly created contexts.
Rung 2	**A2: Cause and Effect** — Students will be able to identify and predict relationships between character behavior and story events and their effects upon other characters or events.	**B2: Classifications** — Students will be able to categorize different aspects of the text or identify and sort categories from a list of topics or details.	**C2: Inference** — Students will be able to use textual clues to read between the lines and make judgments about specific textual events, ideas, or character analysis.	**D2: Summarizing** — Students will be able to provide a synopsis of text sections.	**E2: Expressing Emotion** — Students will be able to articulate their feelings through a variety of media (e.g., song, art, poem, story, essay, speech).	**F2: Thinking About Words** — Students will be able to analyze the use of words within the context as related to the theme of a text.
Rung 1	**A1: Sequencing** — Students will be able to list, in order of importance or occurrence in the text, specific events or plot summaries.	**B1: Details** — Students will be able to list specific details or recall facts related to the text or generate a list of ideas about a specific topic or character.	**C1: Literary Elements** — Students will be able to identify and explain specific story elements such as character, setting, or poetic device.	**D1: Paraphrasing** — Students will be able to restate lines read using their own words.	**E1: Understanding Emotion** — Students will be able to explain how emotion and feeling are conveyed in a text and/or their personal experience.	**F1: Understanding Words** — Students will be able to identify and explain the meaning of figurative language or new vocabulary within the context of a story or poem.

Ladder A: Focus on Implications and Consequences

The goal of Ladder A is to develop prediction and forecasting skills by encouraging students to make connections among the information provided. Starting with sequencing, students learn to recognize basic types of change that occur within a text. Through identifying cause and effect relationships, students then can judge the impact of certain events. Finally, through recognizing consequences and implications, students predict future events as logical and identify both short- and long-term consequences by judging probable outcomes based on data provided. The rungs are as follows:

- **Ladder A, Rung 1, Sequencing:** The lowest rung on the ladder, sequencing, requires students to organize a set of information in order, based on their reading (e.g., List the steps of a recipe in order).
- **Ladder A, Rung 2, Cause and Effect:** The middle rung, cause and effect, requires students to think about relationships and identify what causes certain effects and/or what effects were brought about because of certain causes (e.g., What causes a cake to rise in the oven? What effect does the addition of egg yolks have on a batter?).
- **Ladder A, Rung 3, Consequences and Implications:** The highest rung on Ladder A requires students to think about both short- and long-term events that may happen as a result of an effect they have identified (e.g., What are the short- and long-term consequences of baking at home?). Students learn to draw consequences and implications from the text for application in the real world.

Ladder B: Focus on Generalizations

The goal of Ladder B is to help students develop deductive reasoning skills, moving from the concrete elements in a story to abstract ideas. Students begin by learning the importance of concrete details and how they can be organized. By the top rung, students are able to make general statements spanning a topic or concept. The rungs are as follows:

- **Ladder B, Rung 1, Details:** The lowest rung on Ladder B, details, requires students to list examples or details from what they have read and/or to list examples they know from the real world or have read about (e.g., Make a list of types of transportation. Write as many as you can think of in 2 minutes).

- **Ladder B, Rung 2, Classifications:** The middle rung of Ladder B, classifications, focuses on students' ability to categorize examples and details based on characteristics (e.g., How might we categorize the modes of transportation you identified?). This activity builds students' skills in categorization and classification.
- **Ladder B, Rung 3, Generalizations:** The highest rung on Ladder B, generalizations, requires students to use the list and categories generated at Rungs 1 and 2 to develop two to three general statements that apply to *all* of their examples (e.g., Write three statements about transportation).

Ladder C: Focus on Themes

The goal of Ladder C is to develop literary analysis skills based on an understanding of literary elements. After completing Ladder C, students state the main themes and ideas of the text after identifying setting, characters, and the context of the piece. The rungs for this ladder are as follows:
- **Ladder C, Rung 1, Literary Elements:** While working on the lowest rung of Ladder C, literary elements, students identify and/ or describe the setting or situation in which the reading occurs. This rung also requires students to develop an understanding of a given character by identifying qualities he or she possesses and comparing these qualities to other characters they have encountered in their reading (e.g., In *Goldilocks and the Three Bears*, what is the situation in which Goldilocks finds herself? What qualities do you admire in Goldilocks? What qualities do you find problematic? How is she similar to or different from other fairy tale characters you have encountered?).
- **Ladder C, Rung 2, Inference:** The middle rung of Ladder C, inference, requires students to think through a situation in the text and come to a conclusion based on the information and clues provided (e.g., What evidence exists that Goldilocks ate the porridge? What inferences can you make about the bears' subsequent action?).
- **Ladder C, Rung 3, Theme/Concept:** The highest rung of Ladder C, theme/concept, requires students to state the central idea or theme for a reading. This exercise necessitates that the students explain an idea from the reading that best states what the text means (e.g., How would you rename the fairy tale? Why? What is the overall theme of *Goldilocks and the Three Bears*? Which morals apply to the fairy tale? Why?).

Ladder D: Focus on Creative Synthesis

The goal of Ladder D is to help students develop skills in creative synthesis in order to foster students' creation of new material based on information from the reading. It moves from the level of restating ideas to creating new ideas about a topic or concept. The rungs are as follows:

- **Ladder D, Rung 1, Paraphrasing:** The lowest rung on Ladder D is paraphrasing. This rung requires students to restate a short passage using their own words (e.g., Rewrite the following quotation in your own words: "But as soon as [the slave] came near to Androcles, he recognized his friend, and fawned upon him, and licked his hands like a friendly dog. The emperor, surprised at this, summoned Androcles to him, who told the whole story. Whereupon the slave was pardoned and freed, and the Lion let loose to his native forest.").
- **Ladder D, Rung 2, Summarizing:** Summarizing, the middle rung on Ladder D, requires students to summarize larger sections of text by selecting the most important key points within a passage (e.g., Choose one section of the story and summarize it in five sentences).
- **Ladder D, Rung 3, Creative Synthesis:** The highest rung on Ladder D requires students to create something new using what they have learned from the reading and their synopses of it (e.g., Write another fable about the main idea you identified for this fable using characters, setting, and a plot of your choice).

Ladder E: Focus on Emotional Development

The goal of Ladder E is to help students develop skills in using their emotional intelligence in order to regulate and modulate behavior with respect to learning. It moves from students' understanding of emotion in self and others, to expressing emotion, to channeling emotion for cognitive ends. The rungs are as follows:

- **Ladder E, Rung 1, Understanding Emotion:** The lowest rung on Ladder E is understanding emotion in oneself and others. This requires students to identify emotions in characters and relate them to their own lives (e.g., What feelings does the main character portray throughout the story? How would you compare his temperament to yours?). It also requires them to recognize emotional situations and pinpoint the nature of the emotions involved and what is causing them. Many of the poetry and short story selections are employed to engage students in the use of this ladder.

- **Ladder E, Rung 2, Expressing Emotion:** The middle rung on Ladder E, expressing emotion, asks students to express emotion in response to their reading of various selections (e.g., The main character seems to worry too much. Is worry ever beneficial? Why or why not?). They may often do this in self-selected formats, including poetry or prose. Teachers may want to substitute kinesthetic responses in the form of dance or skits that demonstrate an emotional reaction to the selections.

- **Ladder E, Rung 3, Using Emotion:** The highest rung on Ladder E, using emotion, encourages students to begin regulating emotion for specific purposes (e.g., How does worry impact your life? What steps can you take to minimize worry? Write a personal action plan). In application to poetry, prose, and nonfiction, students need to demonstrate a clear understanding of how to use emotion effectively for accomplishing specific ends, whether through giving a speech or writing a passionate letter in defense of an idea. The deliberate incorporation of emotion in one's communication is stressed.

Ladder F: Focus on Word Study[1]

In *Jacob's Ladder Primary 1* and *Primary 2*, Ladder F focuses on word study. Appropriate for primary readers, the goal of Ladder F is to move students from understanding meanings of words or figurative language to appropriately using words within an applicable context or their own creation.

- **Ladder F, Rung 1, Understanding Words:** The lowest rung on Ladder F is understanding words. It requires students to consider how words are used in the context of the story to promote meaning (e.g., Highlight examples of metaphors in the poem). Through application of language used in the story, students find new examples or uses of literary elements (e.g., personification, symbols, metaphor, simile, idioms) or root words and stems to promote meaning and understanding of words, word families, and figurative uses of language.

- **Ladder F, Rung 2, Thinking About Words:** The middle rung of Ladder F, thinking about words, requires students to think about how the author uses key words or language elements studied in the first rung to enhance the meaning of the story. Students engage in

---

1   In Levels 4 and 5, Ladder F has a focus on metacognition.

analyzing author word choice or deciphering how figurative language enhances the author's message (e.g., How does the author use metaphors to provide images in the reader's mind? Draw a picture of the comparisons).

- **Ladder F, Rung 3, Playing With Words:** The highest rung on Ladder F, playing with words, engages students in reflecting on key words or literary elements and applying them to new situations or contexts. Students are asked to create new poems or stories that incorporate figurative language or new words and word families, to apply the new learning to other writing pieces (e.g., Look outside your school window at an object. How does your selected object resemble a person? Use personification and write at least three sentences to describe your object, giving it human qualities), and to select the most important aspects of language for their own use to meaningfully convey ideas.

Process Skills

Along with the six goals addressed by the ladders, a seventh goal focusing on process skills is incorporated in the *Jacob's Ladder* curriculum. The aim of this goal is to promote learning through interaction and discussion of reading material in the classroom. After completing the ladders and following guidelines for discussion and teacher feedback, students will be able to:

- articulate their understanding of a reading passage using textual support,
- engage in proper dialogue about the meaning of a selection, and
- discuss varied ideas about the intention of a passage both orally and in writing.

Reading Genres and Selections

The reading selections in *Jacob's Ladder Primary 1* include two major genres: short stories (award-winning picture books and fables) and poetry. Each reading has been carefully selected with the primary gifted reader in mind based on key conceptual understandings, appropriate and engaging content, and vividness of grade-appropriate illustrations and supports. Note, however, that many of the selections, especially the picture books, are intended as read-alouds and may not be at the appropriate independent reading level of some students. Students may be able to think critically, but may be unable to read the selected stories fluently. *Jacob's Ladder Primary 1* consists of 20 short stories and 10 poems.

The readings and ladder exercises are designed to move students forward in their understanding of language, reading comprehension, and textual analysis by promoting critical and creative thinking. The vocabulary in each reading is grade-level appropriate; however, when new or unfamiliar words are encountered, they should be covered in class before the readings and ladders are assigned. Themes are appropriate for the students' ages at each grade level and were chosen to complement themes typically seen in texts for each particular level. The short stories and poetry readings with corresponding ladder sets are delineated in Part II. Table 2 outlines all *Jacob's Ladder Primary 1* readings by genre.

Please note that the recommended picture books are *not* included with *Jacob's Ladder Primary 1*. Many award-winning and popular picture books were selected based on their availability in libraries and for purchase online. They are to be secured separately for use with this series.

Research Base

A quasi-experimental study was conducted using *Jacob's Ladder* as a supplementary program for grade 3–5 students in Title I schools. After receiving professional development, teachers were instructed to implement the *Jacob's Ladder* curriculum in addition to their basal reading series and guided reading groups.

Findings from this study (N = 495) suggested that when compared to students who used the basal reader only, those students who were exposed to the *Jacob's Ladder* curriculum showed significant gains in reading comprehension and critical thinking. Likewise, students who used the curriculum showed significant and important growth on curriculum-based assessments that included determining implications and consequences, making inferences, outlining themes and generalizations, and applying creative synthesis. Students reported greater interest in reading and alluded that the curriculum made them "think harder." Teachers reported more in-depth student discussion and personal growth in the ability to ask open-ended questions in reading (Stambaugh, 2012).

Who Should Use *Jacob's Ladder*?

Although the program is targeted for gifted learners and for promising students who need more exposure to higher level thinking skills in read-

TABLE 2
Jacob's Ladder Primary 1 Selections by Genre

Short Stories		Poetry
Ella Sarah Gets Dressed by Margaret Chodos-Irvine**	*Noah's Ark* by Peter Spier*	"Daffodowndilly" by A. A. Milne
Flotsam by David Wiesner*	*There's a Nightmare in My Closet* by Mercer Mayer	"The Crocodile" by Lewis Carroll
The Red Book by Barbara Lehman**	*Ox-Cart Man* by Donald Hall (Author) and Barbara Cooney (Illustrator)*	"Swing Song" by A. A. Milne
Kitten's First Full Moon by Kevin Henkes*	*The Man Who Walked Between the Towers* by Mordicai Gerstein*	"The Four Friends" by A. A. Milne
A Sick Day for Amos McGee by Philip C. Stead (Author) and Erin E. Stead (Illustrator)*	*Paul Bunyan* by Steven Kellogg	"Fire in the Window" by Mary Mapes Dodge
The Hare and the Tortoise originally told by Aesop	*The Girl Who Loved Wild Horses* by Paul Goble*	"A Kitten" by Eleanor Farjeon
Owen by Kevin Henkes**	*Make Way for Ducklings* by Robert McCloskey*	"My Shadow" by Robert Louis Stevenson
Anno's Journey by Mitsumasa Anno	*The Polar Express* by Chris Van Allsburg*	"Little Things" by Ebenezer Cobham Brewer
Doctor De Soto by William Steig***	*The Ants and the Grasshopper* originally told by Aesop	"Mummy Slept Late and Daddy Fixed Breakfast" by John Ciardi
Come Away From the Water, Shirley by John Burningham	*Where the Wild Things Are* by Maurice Sendak*	"Whether the Weather" by Anonymous

*Denotes Caldecott Medal Winner, **Denotes Caldecott Honor Book, *** Denotes Newberry Honor Book

ing, the program may be suitable for other learners as well, including those who are twice-exceptional, students from poverty, and those from different cultural backgrounds (VanTassel-Baska & Stambaugh, 2006b). The reading selections in the program include classic and contemporary literature that has been used at various grade levels with various groups (VanTassel-Baska & Stambaugh, 2006a). Students do not have to read fluently to engage in the *Jacob's Ladder Primary 1* activities. It is recommended that the teacher read many of the selections aloud and promote ongoing discussion with students who have the ability to analyze and think critically about text, even though their independent reading skills may not be at the level of some of the selected materials.

Implementation Considerations

Teachers need to consider certain issues when implementing the *Jacob's Ladder* curriculum. Because modeling, coaching, and feedback appear to enhance student growth in reading and writing (Pressley et al., 2001; Taylor, Peterson, Pearson, & Rodriquez, 2002), it is recommended that teachers review how to complete the task ladders with the entire class at least once, outlining expectations and record-keeping tasks, as well as modeling the process prior to assigning small-group or independent work. As students gain more confidence in the curriculum, teachers should allow more independent work coupled with small-group or paired discussion, and then whole-group sharing with teacher feedback. *Jacob's Ladder* is *not* intended as a worksheet or individual task, but for the facilitation of ongoing discussion and reasoning.

Completing these activities in dyads or small groups will facilitate discussions that stress collaborative reasoning, thereby fostering greater engagement and higher level thinking (Chin, Anderson, & Waggoner, 2001; Pressley et al., 2001; Taylor et al., 2002). The readings and accompanying ladder questions and activities also may be organized into a reading center in the classroom or utilized with reading groups during guided reading for those students who are independent readers. Teachers may also choose to read the selections aloud to students in advanced-level reading groups or to the entire class and solicit responses through methods like think-pair-share, whole-group class discussion, or small-group/individual assignments to be completed prior to engaging in a reading group.

Process of *Jacob's Ladder*

The process of inquiry and feedback, as led and modeled by the teacher, is critical to the success of the program and student mastery of process skills. Teachers need to solicit multiple student responses and encourage dialogue about various perspectives and interpretations of a given text, requiring students to justify their answers with textual support and concrete examples (VanTassel-Baska & Stambaugh, 2006a, 2006b). Sample follow-up questions and prompts such as those listed below can be used by the teacher and posted in the classroom to guide student discussion.

- That's interesting; does anyone have a different idea?
- What in the story makes you say that?
- What do you think the author means by . . . ?
- What do you think are the implications or consequences of . . . ?

- Did anyone view that differently? How?
- Does anyone have a different point of view? Justify your answer.
- In the story I noticed that . . . Do you think that might have significance to the overall meaning?
- I heard someone say that they thought the poem (story) was about . . . What do you think? Justify your answer from the events of the story.
- Do you notice any key words that might be significant? Why?
- Do you notice any words that give you a mental picture? Do those words have significance? What might they symbolize?
- I agree with . . . because . . .
- I had a different idea than . . . because . . .

Beck and McKeown (1998) suggested that academic discourse in reading promotes textual understanding. They recommended guiding students through the text by showing them how to mark key words in a text both on their own and as part of whole-group modeling. Knowing that teacher stance is critical to the process of reasoning and understanding, teachers are encouraged to help students use evidence from the text to justify responses, including turning back in the text to show where ideas were found. Teachers should also model metacognitive approaches by thinking aloud about how one may go about developing an idea or comment, providing annotations or background information as necessary and then synthesizing key ideas expressed during a discussion. This guidance will promote critical thinking when combined with the discourse of also asking targeted, open-ended questions to help students gain understanding for themselves, without being told what to think.

Grouping Students

Jacob's Ladder may be used in a number of different grouping patterns. The program should be introduced initially as a whole-group activity directed by the teacher with appropriate open-ended questions, feedback, and monitoring. After students have examined each type of ladder with teacher guidance, they should be encouraged to use the program by writing ideas independently, sharing with a partner, and then discussing the findings with a group. The dyad approach provides maximal opportunities for student discussion of the readings and collaborative decisions about the answers to questions posed. One purpose of the program is to solicit meaningful discussion of the text, which is best accomplished in small groups of students at similar reading levels (VanTassel-Baska & Little, 2011).

Research continues to support instructional grouping in reading as an important part of successful implementation of a program (Rogers, 2002). Students who are unable to independently read some of the selections for this level may need to have books read aloud to them before discussing ideas with a partner or creating responses. Students may also need to represent their ideas and responses in nontraditional ways, such as drawing and labeling instead of writing, unless writing is a key goal or outcome of the ladder content.

Demonstrating Growth: Pre- and Postassessments and Student Products

The pre- and postassessments included in Appendix A were designed as a diagnostic-prescriptive approach to guide program implementation of *Jacob's Ladder*. The pretest should be administered, scored, and then used to guide student instruction and the selection of readings for varied ability groups. Both the pre- and postassessment and rating scale are included in Appendix A.

In both the pre- and postassessments, students read a short passage and respond to the three questions. Question 1 focuses on reading comprehension through summarizing key events in the story. Question 2 assesses students' knowledge of key themes and ideas through the interpretation or explanation of a fable, and Question 3 examines students' ability to make connections and inferences between the meaning of the text and real-world contexts.

Upon conclusion of the program or as a midpoint check, the posttest may be administered to compare the pretest results and to measure growth in students' responses. These pre-post results could be used as part of a student portfolio, in a parent-teacher conference, or as documentation of curriculum effectiveness and student progress.

Student Feedback and Record Keeping

Teachers will want to check student answers as ladder segments are completed and conduct an individual or small-group consultation to ensure that students understand why their answers may be effective or ineffective. Appendix A also includes a discussion checklist that teachers may use to analyze whether or not students understand key content through group or individual responses that may not be in writing. In order to analyze student responses and progress across the program, teachers need to monitor student performance, providing specific comments about student work to promote growth and understanding of content. Although *Jacob's Ladder Levels 1–5* have answer sheet templates, given the developmental nature of student writing at the primary level, answer sheets are not provided in this book as students may need larger areas or lined paper for recording responses.

Record-keeping sheets for differentiation within the class are provided in Appendix B. On these forms, teachers record student progress on a 3-point scale: 2 (*applies skills very effectively*), 1 (*understands and applies skills*), or a 0 (*needs more practice with the given skill set*) across readings and ladder sets. These forms can be used as part of a diagnostic/prescriptive approach to selecting reading materials and ladders based on student understanding or the need for more practice. Teachers may select readings commensurate with key ladder set skills needed by individual students and then flexibly group those students according to their levels of understanding of a particular ladder thinking skill.

Sample Concluding Activities: Ideas for Grades

Grading the ladders and responses are at the teacher's discretion. Teachers should not overemphasize the lower rungs in graded activities. Lower rungs are intended only as a vehicle to the higher level questions at the top of the ladder. Instead, top-rung questions may be used as a journal prompt or as part of a graded open-ended writing response. Grades also could be given based on guided discussion after students are trained on appropriate ways to discuss literature. Additional ideas for grading are as follows:

- Draw a picture and label it to explain what the story is about.
- Create a symbol to show the meaning of the story. Write two sentences to justify your answer.
- In one word or phrase, what is this story mostly about? Justify your answer using examples from the story.
- Write a poem using similes or metaphors as modeled by the author.
- Pretend you are an illustrator and need to create a drawing for the story or poem that shows what that selection is mostly about. Write a sentence to describe your illustration and why it is the best option.

Time Allotment

Although the time needed to complete *Jacob's Ladder* tasks will vary by student, most lessons should take students 15–30 minutes to read the selection aloud or with a partner and another 20–30 minutes to complete one ladder individually. More time is required for paired student and whole-group discussion of the questions or for specific creative synthesis tasks that involve more writing or researching. Teachers may wish to set aside 2 days each week for focusing on one *Jacob's Ladder* reading and commensurate ladders, especially when introducing the program.

Alignment to Common Core State Standards in English Language Arts

The new Common Core State Standards are K–12 content standards, developed in math and language arts to illustrate the curriculum emphases needed to develop in all students the skills and concepts needed for the 21st century. Adopted by an overwhelming majority of states to date, the standards are organized into key content strands and articulated across all years of schooling. The initiative has been state-based and collaboratively led through two consortia and coordinated by the National Governors Association (NGA) and the Council of Chief State School Officers (CCSSO). Designed by teachers, administrators, and content experts, the standards seek to prepare K–12 students for college and the workplace.

The new standards in language arts are evidence based, aligned with expectations for success in college and the workplace, and informed by the successes and failures of the current standards and international competition demands. They stress rigor, depth, clarity, and coherence, drawing from key national and international reports in mathematics and science. They provide a framework for curriculum development work that remains to be done—although many states are already engaged in the process.

Alignment Approaches to the *Jacob's Ladder Reading Comprehension Program*

Jacob's Ladder exemplifies a model curriculum that addresses the Common Core State Standards in English language arts through several approaches including advanced readings, the use of higher level skills and product demands that address the common core emphases for argument and persuasion directly, and a focus on concept/theme development that is mirrored in the new standards.

There are three major strategies the authors of the *Jacob's Ladder Reading Comprehension Program* have used to accomplish the alignment to the Common Core State Standards.

- *Jacob's Ladder* provides pathways to advance the learning of the Common Core State Standards for gifted learners. Some of the standards do address higher level skills and concepts that should receive focus throughout the years of schooling such as a major emphasis on the skills of argument in language arts. However, there are also more discrete skills that may be clustered across grade levels and compressed around higher level skills and concepts for more efficient mastery by the gifted. The *Jacob's Ladder* curriculum series moves students from lower order comprehension skills in reading to higher order critical reading and thinking skills within the same set of activities, thus advancing their higher level learning in verbal areas.
- The program provides differentiated task demands to address specific Common Core State Standards.
- Standards, such as the research standard in the new common core English language arts standards, lend themselves to differentiated interpretation by demonstrating what a typical learner might be able to do at a given stage of development versus what a gifted learner might be able to do. The differentiated examples in *Jacob's Ladder* show greater complexity and creativity, using a more advanced curriculum base. In language arts, typical learners might learn the literary elements and practice their application across grades K–8, while gifted learners show mastery of the relationship of the parts of literary elements through the carefully constructed ladders that explore these elements in an integrated way at all levels with increasingly complex and creative questions and activities.
- *Jacob's Ladder* features interdisciplinary product demands, based on the Common Core State Standards in English language arts.

Because English language arts standards can be grouped together in application, much of the project work in *Jacob's Ladder* connects to the new Common Core State Standards and shows how multiple standards can be addressed across content areas. For example, research projects are designed to address the research standard in English language arts by delineating a product demand for research on an issue, beginning by asking researchable questions and using multiple sources to answer them and then representing the findings in tables, graphs, and other visual displays that are explained in the text and presented to an audience with implications for a plan of action. This approach to interdisciplinary work across math, science, and language arts is a central part of the *Jacob's Ladder* program at the upper elementary and middle school levels with developmentally appropriate connections at the primary and intermediate levels of *Jacob's Ladder* in the early grades. Regular connections to social studies and the arts are embedded at all levels of the program as appropriate to selected readings.

References

Beck, I. L., & McKeown, M. G. (1998). Comprehension: The sine qua non of reading. In S. Patton & M. Holmes (Eds.), *The keys to literacy* (pp. 40–52). Washington, DC: Council for Basic Education.

Bransford, J. D., Brown, A. L., & Cocking, R. R. (2000). *How people learn: Brain, mind, experience.* Washington, DC: National Academy Press.

Chin, C. A., Anderson, R. C., & Waggoner, M. A. (2001). Patterns of discourse in two kinds of literature discussion. *Reading Research Quarterly, 30,* 378–411.

Guthrie, J. T., Schafer, W. D., & Huang, C. (2001). Benefits of opportunity to read and balanced instruction on the NAEP. *Journal of Educational Research, 94,* 145–162.

Pressley, M., Wharton-McDonald, R., Allington, R., Block, C. C., Morrow, L., Tracey, D., . . . Woo, D. (2001). A study of effective first-grade literacy instruction. *Scientific Studies of Reading, 5,* 35–58.

Rawson, K. A., Dunlosky, J., & Thiede, K. W. (2000). The rereading effect: Metacomprehension accuracy improves across reading trials. *Memory & Cognition, 28*(6), 1004.

Rogers, K. (2002). *Re-forming gifted education: How parents and teachers can match the program to the child.* Scottsdale, AZ: Great Potential Press.

Stambaugh, T. (2012). *Effects of the Jacob's Ladder Reading Comprehension Program.* Manuscript submitted for publication.

Taylor, B. M., Pearson, P. D., Peterson, D. S., & Rodriguez, M. C. (2003). Reading growth in high-poverty classrooms: The influence of teacher practices that encourage cognitive engagement in literacy learning. *The Elementary School Journal, 104,* 3–30.

Taylor, B. M., Peterson, D. S., Pearson, P. D., & Rodriguez, M. C. (2002). Looking inside classrooms: Reflecting on the "how" as well as the "what" in effective reading instruction. *Reading Teacher, 56,* 270–279.

Tivnan, T., & Hemphill, L. (2005). Comparing four literacy reform models in high-poverty schools: Patterns of first grade achievement. *Elementary School Journal, 105,* 419–443.

VanTassel-Baska, J., & Stambaugh, T. (2006a). *Comprehensive curriculum for gifted learners* (3rd ed.). Needham Heights, MA: Allyn & Bacon.

VanTassel-Baska, J., & Stambaugh, T. (2006b). Project Athena: A pathway to advanced literacy development for children of poverty. *Gifted Child Today, 29*(2), 58–65.

VanTassel-Baska, J., & Little, C. (Eds.). (2011). *Content-based curriculum for gifted learners* (2nd ed.). Waco, TX: Prufrock Press.

Villaume, S. K., & Brabham, E. G. (2002). Comprehension instruction: Beyond strategies. *The Reading Teacher, 55,* 672–676.

Part II: Readings and Student Ladder Sets

Chapter 1: Short Stories

Chapter 2: Poetry

CHAPTER

1

Short Stories

Chapter 1 includes information on the selected readings or the readings themselves and accompanying question sets for each short story selection. Each selection is followed by two or three sets of questions; each set is aligned to one of the six sets of ladder skills.

For *Jacob's Ladder Primary 1*, the skills covered by each selection are as follows:

Ella Sarah Gets Dressed

by Margaret Chodos-Irvine
Caldecott Honor Book

Although her mother, father, and older sister advise her to dress in a more conventional manner, Ella Sarah persists in wearing the striking and unusual outfit of her own choosing. Her friends arrive at her house also wearing their handpicked, flamboyant outfits, showing Ella Sarah that she picked the perfect ensemble.

Consequences and Implications

A3

What are the positive and negative consequences of selecting your own clothes? How do those compare to Ella Sarah's situation?

Cause and Effect

A2

What caused Ella Sarah to want to wear her special outfit? Explain your answer.

Sequencing

A1

Sequence the events in the story that led to Ella Sarah getting to wear what she wanted. Include no more than four events. Be prepared to share your reasons for choosing the events.

ELLA SARAH GETS DRESSED

Using Emotion

E3

Draw a picture about a time you wanted to do something on your own. How did you feel? Use colors to outline your feelings. Be ready to tell a partner how the colors you selected show the feelings you want your partner to feel when he or she looks at them.

Expressing Emotion

E2

How do the colors used in the story make you feel? Explain your answer. Do the colors match the words and events in the story?

Understanding Emotion

E1

How does the author use pictures and color to show how Ella Sarah reacted when she wasn't permitted to wear what she wanted?

ELLA SARAH GETS DRESSED

Flotsam

by David Wiesner
Caldecott Medal Winner

When a curious young boy goes to the beach in search of items that have been washed ashore, he discovers an underwater camera. Upon developing its film, he finds a treasure greater than he could have ever imagined: The photographs have many layers of interesting pictures within, exposing the wonders of the deep sea.

Consequences and Implications

A3

What were the implications of the boy finding the camera? How do you know?

Cause and Effect

A2

What effect did the camera have on the children who found it? Explain your answer using information from the story.

Sequencing

A1

What events happened before the boy found the camera? Which pictures in the story support your answer?

FLOTSAM

Theme/Concept

C3

What meaning is conveyed by the use of close-ups and far away shots? How does this technique help us see the author's intent?

Inference

C2

Why did the boy take a picture of himself and then throw the camera back into the water? Support your answer using other pictures in the story.

Literary Elements

C1

How does the author use photos to tell a story? Why are some photos close up and others far away? How does that help the reader understand what is going on?

FLOTSAM

Creative Synthesis

D3

Think about the world around you and all of the things that happen in it. Create a picture story of at least five pictures from different points of view that illustrate what is going on in the treetops, grass, or other areas of your world that you cannot see. Compare your drawings with the drawings in the book.

Summarizing

D2

Select one of your favorite pages of the story and summarize why it is your favorite.

Paraphrasing

D1

In your own words, tell what happened after the boy threw the camera into the ocean.

FLOTSAM

The Red Book

by Barbara Lehman

Caldecott Honor Book

This book about a book exposes both the main character and readers to new parts of the world. The main character, a young schoolgirl, finds a magical red book that has the ability to connect people from remote distances, allowing her to develop a friendship with a boy who is far away.

A3

Consequences and Implications

Why do you think the author made the book red instead of another color?

A2

Cause and Effect

What effect did the book have on the two characters in the story? Show the pictures that help you answer the question.

A1

Sequencing

Tell in order the three most important events in the story. Compare and explain your ideas with a partner's.

THE RED BOOK

Theme/Concept

C3

Is this book about imagination or friendship? Explain your ideas.

Inference

C2

Did the boy really exist or was it part of the red book? Explain your answer.

Literary Elements

C1

How does the author use pictures to tell a story? What features make the pictures tell a story?

THE RED BOOK

THE RED BOOK

Creative Synthesis

D3

Create a wordless book that tells a story. Ask your friends if they can tell what happens in your story by only your drawings.

Summarizing

D2

What happened after the girl floated away with the balloons? Tell a partner and compare ideas.

Paraphrasing

D1

Tell what happened immediately after the girl sees the map. How do you know?

Kitten's First Full Moon

by Kevin Henkes
Caldecott Medal Winner

When Kitten sees the full moon for the first time, she mistakenly believes it is a bowl of milk. Determined to drink its delicious contents, she makes many attempts to reach the bowl, leaving her tired, wet, and hungry.

Theme/Concept

C3

What lesson did you learn from the story? Explain how you arrived at your answer.

Inference

C2

What character trait made Kitten continue to try to reach the moon? Explain your answer using information from the story.

Literary Elements

C1

How would you describe Kitten's personality? Why?

KITTEN'S FIRST FULL MOON

Using Emotion

E3

Draw a picture that shows how Kitten must have felt before and after she got her bowl of milk. Use special colors to show what her mood might have been. Write or dictate a sentence to explain why you chose the color you did to illustrate Kitten's two moods.

Expressing Emotion

E2

Think about a time when you failed at something you tried. Tell a partner what happened and how you felt. Draw a picture that shows your emotions and write or dictate a sentence to explain them.

Understanding Emotion

E1

What emotions do you think Kitten felt when she kept failing at her attempts to lick the moon? Use examples from the book to share your ideas.

KITTEN'S FIRST FULL MOON

Playing With Words

F3

Add one more page to the book with illustrations and words that show another failed attempt of Kitten trying to reach the moon. Use action words to illustrate Kitten's failed attempts.

Thinking About Words

F2

On certain pages, the author uses the same verb over and over to explain Kitten's actions. For example, " . . . she climbed and climbed and climbed . . ." Why would the author do this? What does it make the reader think or imagine?

Understanding Words

F1

The author uses many different verbs (action words) to help readers understand how Kitten moved in an attempt to get to the moon. Make a list of those verbs and define the ones you don't know. Draw a picture of each action.

KITTEN'S FIRST FULL MOON

A Sick Day for Amos McGee

by Philip C. Stead (Author) and Erin E. Stead (Illustrator)
Caldecott Medal Winner

Zookeeper Amos McGee always makes time to visit his friends who live at the zoo until the day he stays home because he is sick. The animals, realizing what a good friend Amos has always been, decide it's their turn to do something nice for their sick friend. They leave the zoo to go to Amos' house, where they take care of him and keep him company through the day and night.

Consequences and Implications

A3

What are the positive and negative consequences of being a friend? Use examples from the story to explain your answer.

Cause and Effect

A2

What effect did Amos have on the animals? How do you know?

Sequencing

A1

List or draw the four most important events in the story. Be prepared to explain why the events you chose were most important.

A SICK DAY FOR AMOS MCGEE

Theme/Concept

C3

Some people say this story is about friendship. Others say it is about sacrifice. Which one word best describes this story in your opinion? Explain your answer by citing specific examples.

Inference

C2

What made Amos a friend to the animals? What made the animals friends to Amos? Who was a better friend? Why?

Literary Elements

C1

How would you describe Amos McGee's personality?

A SICK DAY FOR AMOS MCGEE

Creative Synthesis

D3

Write your name down the side of a piece of paper in large letters. Beside each letter, write as many adjectives that begin with that letter that describe you as a friend. On a separate piece of paper, create a Venn diagram that compares and contrasts your qualities with Amos'. What do you have in common? What is different?

Summarizing

D2

Summarize in one sentence the lesson you learned from this story.

Paraphrasing

D1

In your own words, explain what happened when the animals found out Amos was not coming to work.

A SICK DAY FOR AMOS MCGEE

The Hare and the Tortoise

Originally told by Aesop

The Hare was once boasting of his speed before the other animals. "I have never yet been beaten," said he, "when I put forth my full speed. I challenge any one here to race with me."

The Tortoise said quietly, "I accept your challenge."

"That is a good joke," said the Hare; "I could dance round you all the way."

"Keep your boasting till you've won," answered the Tortoise. "Shall we race?"

So a course was fixed and a start was made. The Hare darted almost out of sight at once, but soon stopped and, to show his contempt for the Tortoise, lay down to have a nap. The Tortoise plodded on and plodded on, and when the Hare awoke from his nap, he saw the Tortoise just near the winning-post and could not run up in time to save the race.

Then the Tortoise said: "Slow but steady progress wins the race."

Generalizations

B3

Write at least two statements that are true about all winners based on your details and categories.

Classifications

B2

Use your words from the details section of this ladder and classify them into three or more categories.

Details

B1

In this fable, the turtle won by being persistent. Brainstorm as many qualities you can think of that help you win.

THE HARE AND THE TORTOISE

Theme/Concept

C3

What is meant by the tortoise's statement:
"Slow but steady progress wins the race"?

Inference

C2

What makes this fable unusual or
unexpected? How do you know?

Literary Elements

C1

Write three words that best describe the tortoise
and three words that best describe the hare.
Use new words not included in the fable.

THE HARE AND THE TORTOISE

Playing With Words

F3

Create your own ironic situation and write, draw, or tell a partner. Be ready to defend how your new situation is ironic.

Thinking About Words

F2

Think about another story you have heard about or read that uses irony. Draw or tell about it.

Understanding Words

F1

Irony is sometimes used to make stories more exaggerated, unusual, or comical. Irony is when what is expected is different than what actually happens. How is this story ironic?

THE HARE AND THE TORTOISE

Owen

by Kevin Henkes
Caldecott Honor Book

When Owen's nosy neighbor, Mrs. Tweezers, intimates that Owen is too old for his favorite blanket Fuzzy, his parents try to get him to give it up before he starts school. When their many efforts fail, they finally come up with a solution that makes everyone happy.

Consequences and Implications

A3

What are the positive and negative consequences of the mother's solution for Owen and his blanket? Explain your answer.

Cause and Effect

OWEN

A2

What effect do you think carrying the blanket had on Owen? How do you know?

Sequencing

A1

What three most important events, in order, happened to cause Owen's mother to come up with a new idea for his blanket? Why are the three events you chose most important?

Theme/Concept

C3

Owen's mother was creative in her approach to Owen's problem. How did she show creativity? How is that different from Mrs. Tweezers' approach?

Inference

C2

Why did Mrs. Tweezers continue to tell the family about ways to help Owen get rid of his blanket? Why didn't she say anything at the end of the story?

Literary Elements

C1

Think about people you know in real life. Who is most like Owen's mother? Mrs. Tweezers? Owen? Explain your answers using information from the story.

OWEN

Using Emotion

E3

What are the positive and negative things you experienced when going to school for the first time? How did you find comfort? Write a letter to Owen giving him advice about school.

Expressing Emotion

E2

Owen was comforted by his blanket. Find at least five different ways Owen is comforted by his blanket, and then pretend you are Owen. What toy or other item did you have that comforted you when you were younger? Tell your friend a story about it and then describe how your story compares to Owen's.

Understanding Emotion

E1

How did Owen feel when he was told he had to be a big boy and give up his blanket? What evidence supports your answer?

OWEN

Anno's Journey*

by Mitsumasa Anno

This book records in drawings the author's journey through northern Europe and his impressions of the land, the people at work and play, and their art, architecture, folklore, and fairy tales.

*Other books by Anno may be substituted here, with only a few changes in the ladder questions as needed.

Consequences and Implications

A3

What are the implications of telling a story through pictures only? What would words provide to or take away from the story?

Cause and Effect

A2

What is the effect of Anno's riding closer into the town? List everything you see in the succeeding pictures.

Sequencing

A1

Look throughout the book. Create words to accompany the first three pictures.

ANNO'S JOURNEY

Generalizations

B3 What are the ideas about village life that you come to understand from viewing this series of scenes within the picture? Name at least three.

Classifications

B2 How would you categorize the scenes that are depicted? What title might you give each of them?

Details

B1 Describe the scene in the fifth picture from the end of the book. How many scenes are included? What are the different scenes portraying?

ANNO'S JOURNEY

D3

Creative Synthesis

Create a written story that depicts a journey you have taken. Organize it, using *Anno's Journey* as a model.

D2

Summarizing

Provide a short recap of the journey to include in a local newspaper.

D1

Paraphrasing

In your own words, describe the changes in scenes that Anno experiences in the book.

ANNO'S JOURNEY

Doctor De Soto

by William Steig
Newbery Honor Book

Doctor De Soto, a mouse dentist, helps various animals by treating their toothaches—except those, of course, with a taste for mice. When a fox comes to him one day in great pain, Doctor De Soto is unsure what to do. A kind-hearted mouse, he wants to help the poor fox, but how can he ensure his safety when doing so?

 Jacob's Ladder Reading Comprehension Program Primary 1 © Prufrock Press • This page may be photocopied or reproduced with permission for single classroom use.

Consequences and Implications

A3

This story demonstrates the resourcefulness of the De Sotos in the face of danger. What problem-solving approaches do they use to protect themselves? What is the consequence of their plan on the fox?

Cause and Effect

A2

What is the effect of having the fox as a dental patient? Think of all of the issues associated with this situation.

Sequencing

A1

Sequence the story by listing the major events that occur.

DOCTOR DE SOTO

Theme/Concept

C3

What might you rename the story, based on your understanding of the major ideas?

Inference

C2

What inference do the De Sotos make when they hear the fox mumbling " . . . with just a pinch of salt"? Are they right?

Literary Elements

C1

The author does a good job with the characterization of the De Sotos. What qualities do they exhibit? Make a list and share where each quality is exemplified in the book.

DOCTOR DE SOTO

 Jacob's Ladder Reading Comprehension Program Primary 1 © Prufrock Press • This page may be photocopied or reproduced with permission for single classroom use.

DOCTOR DE SOTO

Creative Synthesis

D3

Create an alternative ending for the story.
What might have happened to the De Sotos?
Dictate the new ending to your teacher and
draw a picture illustrating the event.

Summarizing

D2

Tell the story, highlighting the
major events that happen.

Paraphrasing

D1

In your own words, describe how the fox was tricked.

Come Away From the Water, Shirley

by John Burningham

When Shirley's family goes to the beach one day, her imagination runs wild, taking her on a dangerous journey involving pirates and buried treasure. All the while, her parents caution her with familiar parental warnings, highlighting the different ways in which parents and children experience such an excursion.

Generalizations

B3

What statements can you make about Shirley that are supported by your list and categories?

Classifications

B2

Categorize your list with respect to qualities Shirley exhibits.

Details

B1

What are the details you know about Shirley based on the pictures and the text? Make a list.

COME AWAY FROM THE WATER, SHIRLEY

Theme/Concept

C3

The concept of a fantasy life is very real in this story. How does the author show the reader Shirley's fantasy? What role does she play? What acts does she perform?

Inference

C2

What is your explanation of the differences in the commentary on the left side of the page and the pictures on the right? Why are they so different?

Literary Elements

C1

The plot of Shirley's adventure with the pirates is not written out. Please do so, using the pictures as your basis. Why is a pirate ship a good setting for the story?

COME AWAY FROM THE WATER, SHIRLEY

D3 — Creative Synthesis

This book depends on the wonderful differences in perception of reality experienced by Shirley and her parents. Create a series of eight panels that show perceptions you have that are different from your parents'. Think of ordinary life events on one side and your fantasies about something on the other. Draw the panels and dictate captions or dialogue as appropriate.

D2 — Summarizing

What is the story being told? Retell it in a paragraph or dictate it to your teacher.

D1 — Paraphrasing

In your own words, paraphrase Shirley's fantasy story.

COME AWAY FROM THE WATER, SHIRLEY

Noah's Ark

by Peter Spier
Caldecott Medal Winner

This picture book, depicting the loading and unloading of the ark, is a marvelous retelling in pictures of the Biblical story.

Consequences and Implications

A3

What is the implication of Noah's releasing the white dove? What does the dove represent in the story?

Cause and Effect

A2

What are the effects of the storm on the ark? List out all that you notice in the relevant pictures.

Sequencing

A1

Describe what happens in the book's storm sequence. Order the events that occur.

NOAH'S ARK

Theme/Concept

C3

Select one of the animal pairs on the ark and create a story that illustrates a particular human quality about them or their fortunes. You have now created a personification of animals by giving them human traits.

Inference

C2

What idea do we derive from Noah's act of saving the animals? Why does he do it? What impact does it eventually have on the world?

Literary Elements

C1

Creating a rhyme scheme or rhyming words is an important literary element. Identify rhyming words in the written section and record them in a chart. Identify a pattern for each.

Rhyming Words	Pattern

NOAH'S ARK

Creative Synthesis

D3

Write captions for each picture in the book that reveals the action of the story. Create lines that rhyme if you like. Use the existing rhymed lines as a model.

Summarizing

D2

Summarize or retell the story in prose form instead of the poetry found on the second page.

Paraphrasing

D1

In your own words, describe what is happening on the page opposite the rhyming commentary.

NOAH'S ARK

There's a Nightmare in My Closet

by Mercer Mayer

After spending countless nights afraid of the nightmare in his closet, a boy gathers his courage (along with a small army of toy soldiers, a cannon, and a popgun) to confront his fear, finally realizing that the nightmare is not so terrifying after all.

Generalizations

B3

What generalizations could you state that could become rules for handling nightmares, based on the story?

Classifications

B2

How would you characterize the different approaches of confrontation? Which one is most effective and why?

Details

B1

What details of confronting the nightmare does the author share?

THERE'S A NIGHTMARE IN MY CLOSET

Creative Synthesis

D3

This story reflects a little boy's willingness to confront his nightmares and take charge of them. Create a poem that reflects a similar attitude toward another fear you may have.

Summarizing

D2

Tell the story from the point of view of the nightmare. How is your story different from the original?

Paraphrasing

D1

In your own words, how does the author help the reader accept nightmares?

THERE'S A NIGHTMARE IN MY CLOSET

Ox-Cart Man

by Donald Hall (Author) and Barbara Cooney (Illustrator)
Caldecott Medal Winner

Set roughly in 19th-century New England, this book follows the day-to-day life of one family throughout the changing seasons, highlighting what each of the family members does to contribute to the family's well being.

Consequences and Implications

A3

Predict what the next events in the storyline about the ox-cart man and his family would be. Write (or dictate) two more pages in the style of the author that you could add to the end of the book.

Cause and Effect

A2

Why do the ox-cart man and his family work so hard in the winter, spring, summer, and fall?

Sequencing

A1

Pick one month out of the fall, one month out of the winter, one month out of the spring, and one month out of the summer, and write down events people might do in those months, using the author's version as a model.

OX-CART MAN

Name: _____ Date: _____

Theme/Concept

C3

How does this story illustrate the concept of bartering (trading goods or services for things you need)?

Inference

C2

How would you describe the relationship of the family members to each other? What evidence supports your inference?

Literary Elements

C1

What are the human qualities of the ox-cart man? Write specific examples.

Playing With Words

F3

Retell the story of the first four pages without using repetition of any words or phrases. How does it sound different? Why?

Thinking About Words

F2

Why do you think the author uses anaphora (the repetition of specific phrases) in this story? How does this device relate to the theme of the story?

Understanding Words

F1

List all of the words or specific phrases that appear more than twice on a page.

OX-CART MAN

The Man Who Walked Between the Towers

by Mordicai Gerstein
Caldecott Medal Winner

Using lyrical text and beautiful illustrations, this book recreates French aerialist Philippe Petit's 1974 tightrope walk between the World Trade Center towers, telling the daring story of how, with the help of his friends, he was able to achieve such an amazing and dangerous feat.

A3

Consequences and Implications

The illustrator of the book uses an aerial (bird's eye) perspective. What are the implications of the illustrator using an aerial perspective? Choose your three favorite pictures in the book and describe.

A2

Cause and Effect

Philippe is arrested after he finishes his walk. Do you think his sentencing was fair, given his crime? What effect did his sentence have on him?

A1

Sequencing

Make a list of everything that Philippe had to do in order to accomplish his feat on the tightrope. Sequence the steps in his preparation.

THE MAN WHO WALKED BETWEEN THE TOWERS

Generalizations

B3

If you were to rename the book, what would you call it, and why?

Classifications

B2

Categorize the scenes that Philippe sees as he crosses the wire.

Details

B1

Describe the scene that appears on the title page of the book. What details are important for understanding the story?

THE MAN WHO WALKED BETWEEN THE TOWERS

Using Emotion

E3

In your own words, explain how Philippe felt while he was on the high-wire. Describe something you have done that produced the same feeling.

Expressing Emotion

E2

Turn to the page where Philippe is lying on the wire looking up at the bird in the sky. Describe the different emotions you see in the scene and the emotions you have as you look at it.

Understanding Emotion

E1

What risks did Philippe take in the story? How does this story make you feel about taking risks?

THE MAN WHO WALKED BETWEEN THE TOWERS

Paul Bunyan
by Steven Kellogg

As the largest baby ever born in Maine, lumberjack Paul Bunyan's unusual size and strength bring him a life full of many fantastic adventures and lead to the creation of several of America's most well-known geographic features.

Generalizations

B3

What are some statements you can make
about Paul Bunyan, based on his work?

Classifications

B2

Make a list of all of the projects he completes in the
book. How would you categorize his many projects?

Details

B1

What details of Paul's early life
prepare you for his later feats?

PAUL BUNYAN

Theme/Concept

C3

The concept of "building" is central to this story. What is the evidence that Paul was a genius at getting things built?

Inference

C2

Why was Babe depressed toward the end of the story? How did Paul help him overcome it?

Literary Elements

C1

What is a hero? Look at its meaning in the dictionary. Paul is one of many heroes described as responsible for making the wilderness more habitable. What qualities of a hero does he exhibit?

PAUL BUNYAN

Creative Synthesis

D3

Tell the story of another hero like Paul Bunyan. Complete a drawing of the hero you choose, showing details that you describe in the story. (You may want to research your hero on the Internet by typing in his or her name.)

Summarizing

D2

What is the story of Paul Bunyan in a few sentences?

Paraphrasing

D1

In your own words, what are Paul's most important qualities?

PAUL BUNYAN

The Girl Who Loved Wild Horses

by Paul Goble
Caldecott Medal Winner

After a young Native American girl gets lost in the mountains during a big storm, she befriends a wild horse and lives with its herd. Although happy to see her family and tribe when she finally finds them, she deeply misses the wild horses and falls ill, realizing that she would prefer to stay and live among the herd where she is truly happy and free. Her parents condone her wish and she departs with her animal friends, returning once a year to see her people.

Consequences and Implications

A3 What happened because the girl went away to be among the horses? What ultimately happened to her?

Cause and Effect

A2 What was the impact on the girl when she returned to the Native American village? What caused her illness?

Sequencing

A1 What was the series of events that led to the girl's disappearance?

THE GIRL WHO LOVED WILD HORSES

Name: _____ Date: _____

Theme/Concept

C3

The concept of loyalty is central to this story. Give examples of types of loyalty explored in the story. Complete the following chart on your own paper.

Type of Loyalty	Story Example

Inference

C2

What do you think happened to the girl? Where would Horse People come from?

Literary Elements

C1

In this story, the horses take on the characteristics of human beings as they are described. Name some of these qualities. What qualities did the girl exhibit? Are there any common ones? List them and comment on how they are the same.

Creative Synthesis

D3

The story ends with two Native American poems. Create your own poem, using them as models, to describe horses you have seen or know.

Summarizing

D2

Summarize the story of the Native American girl. What does her life symbolize or represent, do you think?

Paraphrasing

D1

In your own words, describe the action in the buffalo hunt picture at the beginning of the book. Now describe the buffalo picture near the end of the book. What do you see that is similar? What is different?

THE GIRL WHO LOVED WILD HORSES

Make Way for Ducklings

by Robert McCloskey
Caldecott Medal Winner

Mr. and Mrs. Mallard arrive in Boston in search of a safe place to raise their offspring and settle on an island on the Charles River. After the eight ducklings hatch, Mr. Mallard decides to take a trip to see what the rest of the river looks like and instructs Mrs. Mallard to meet him in the Boston Public Garden in one week. When Mrs. Mallard and her eight ducklings get stuck on a busy street along the way, a kind policeman stops traffic and helps the ducklings make it safely to the Public Garden—the home they just might be looking for.

Consequences and Implications

A3

The entire story is set in Boston, MA, and takes place along the Charles River that runs through the city. What were the consequences of the ducklings leaving their safe haven and marching down the street in Boston?

Cause and Effect

A2

What was the effect on the police department of the duck movement?

Sequencing

A1

Sequence the story from the beginning to the end by the major events that occur.

MAKE WAY FOR DUCKLINGS

Generalizations

B3

Based on your list of what goes wrong for the ducklings in the story, create a set of rules for them to follow.

Classifications

B2

What are the categories of concern for the ducklings?

Details

B1

Make a list of what goes wrong for the ducklings in their life in Boston.

MAKE WAY FOR DUCKLINGS

Creative Synthesis

D3

Create your own story about animals living in a big city near you. Use the structure of the book as a guide. Draw a picture of your animals to illustrate the story. What is your title? Be sure it conveys a central action in the story as is the case with *Make Way for Ducklings*.

Summarizing

D2

Summarize the story by creating a timeline of events.

Paraphrasing

D1

Robert McCloskey was a man who drew ducks for a long time—years, in fact—before he wrote and illustrated this book in 1941 and received the Caldecott Medal as the most distinguished picture book for children in that year. In your own words, describe the power of McCloskey's pictures to convey the story. Select one that you really like and indicate its features.

MAKE WAY FOR DUCKLINGS

The Polar Express*

by Chris Van Allsburg
Caldecott Medal Winner

An adult storyteller recounts one Christmas Eve long ago when, after lying awake at night, he is taken on a magical train ride with other children to the North Pole to receive a special gift from Santa Claus.

*This book should be used between the Thanksgiving and Christmas holidays to obtain maximum effect.

Consequences and Implications

A3

What were the implications of the boy's trip on Christmas morning?

Cause and Effect

A2

What kind of effect did Van Allsburg's illustrations have on you? What was your favorite one and why?

Sequencing

A1

By using a train to sequence events, the author has been very effective in telling his story. What are the different ways that Van Allsburg depicts the train from its first to its last appearance in the story?

THE POLAR EXPRESS

Generalizations

B3

What general ideas do you take away from the ride in *The Polar Express*? What was best about it, based on your details?

Classifications

B2

How would you classify the details you have identified?

Details

B1

Provide as many details as you can about the ride that the boy takes on the Polar Express.

THE POLAR EXPRESS

Theme/Concept

C3

The importance of holding fast to dreams is a central idea in this story. What aspects of the dream are important to the boy in the story?

Inference

C2

Why do you think the narrator's parents couldn't hear the bell? Why do you think his sister Sarah couldn't hear it after a number of years?

Literary Elements

C1

This Christmas story uses a dream journey that is depicted on the pages of the book to illustrate what happens to the narrator. What devices does the author use to let us know it is a dream?

THE POLAR EXPRESS

The Ants and the Grasshopper

Originally told by Aesop

The Ants were spending a fine winter's day drying grain collected in the summertime. A Grasshopper, perishing with famine, passed by and earnestly begged for a little food. The Ants inquired of him, "Why did you not treasure up food during the summer?" He replied, "I had not leisure enough. I passed the days in singing." They then said in derision: "If you were foolish enough to sing all the summer, you must dance supperless to bed in the winter."

Consequences and Implications

A3 What are the short-term and long-term consequences of playing around instead of working?

Cause and Effect

A2 What effect did Grasshopper's behavior have on the Ants? How do you know?

Sequencing

A1 Sequence the events of Grasshopper's preparation for winter.

THE ANTS AND THE GRASSHOPPER

Theme/Concept

C3

What one word or phrase best describes this fable? Justify your answer.

Inference

C2

What does the phrase "If you were foolish enough to sing all the summer, you must dance supperless to bed in the winter" mean?

Literary Elements

C1

Why do you think the author used ants and grasshoppers as the main characters?

THE ANTS AND THE GRASSHOPPER

Where the Wild Things Are

by Maurice Sendak
Caldecott Medal Winner

Max, a mischievous little boy, is sent to bed without his supper one night. His room is transformed into another land, and he sails to a place where wild things live. These wild things are giant, odd-looking creatures, and in this world Max becomes their king.

Name: _____ Date: _____

Generalizations

B3

What does the story suggest about imagination?

Classifications

B2

How would you categorize Max's adventures?

Details

B1

What evidence in the story suggests
that Max had a great imagination?

WHERE THE WILD THINGS ARE

D3

Creative Synthesis

The author/illustrator won an award for his drawings. Why do you think that is so? Select one of your favorite pictures in the book and tell a friend at least five reasons why that picture is a good one.

D2

Summarizing

Summarize Max's adventure in his new land.

D1

Paraphrasing

In your own words, tell why Max was sent to his room.

WHERE THE WILD THINGS ARE

Using Emotion

E3

Was Max's way of handling his punishment positive or negative? Explain your answer.

Expressing Emotion

E2

Think about a time you were in trouble for something. How did you handle it? How is that different or the same as Max?

Understanding Emotion

E1

Why do you think Max used his imagination when he got into trouble? Why did he make himself king of all wild things?

WHERE THE WILD THINGS ARE

CHAPTER 2

Poetry

Chapter 2 focuses on selections of children's poems and the accompanying question sets for each poem. Each selection is followed by two or three sets of questions; each set is aligned to one of the six sets of ladder skills.

For *Jacob's Ladder Primary 1*, the skills covered by each selection are as follows:

Daffodowndilly

by A. A. Milne

She wore her yellow sun-bonnet,
She wore her greenest gown;
She turned to the south wind
And curtsied up and down.
She turned to the sunlight
And shook her yellow head,
And whispered to her neighbour:
"Winter is dead."

 Jacob's Ladder Reading Comprehension Program Primary 1 © Prufrock Press • This page may be photocopied or reproduced with permission for single classroom use.

Consequences and Implications

A3

What are the implications of the actions the girl takes for herself, her family, and her neighborhood? For example, what might she do now that winter is over, what might her family do, and what might her neighborhood do?

Cause and Effect

A2

What will be the effect of the girl telling her neighbor about the seasonal change?

Sequencing

A1

List the sequence of actions that the little girl in the poem makes.

DAFFODOWNDILLY

Theme/Concept

C3

Create a poem using "Daffodowndilly" as a model that expresses your feelings about the coming of a particular season. You may use key words from this poem, how the words are arranged, and other devices you see the poet has employed. Please end your poem with a line that names the season you are commenting on.

Inference

C2

What feelings does the poem cause you to have? How do you think "she" in the poem felt? What in the poem makes you think so?

Literary Elements

C1

The choice of words and images in poetry tell the story. What colors does the poet use in the poem? Why do you think he chose those colors? Why do you think the girl curtsied to the south wind?

DAFFODOWNDILLY

Playing With Words

F3

Write a description of a season, using colors to portray it. (You may type the story or dictate it to your teacher.) Try to describe images of yourself in the poem reacting to the season. Read your description aloud and think about how it could be improved. What words might you change?

Thinking About Words

F2

What is the setting of the poem? How do you know? Why is the place it occurs important to understanding the poem?

Understanding Words

F1

What are the rhyming words in the poem? (Clue: Look at the words at the end of a line.) Create three pairs of rhyming words you could use in a poem. Sometimes poets use a rhyming scheme to apply rhyming words. Which lines in this poem rhyme? Are there other schemes of rhyme that could be applied?

DAFFODOWNDILLY

The Crocodile

by Lewis Carroll

How doth the little crocodile
Improve his shining tail,
And pour the waters of the Nile
On every golden scale!

How cheerfully he seems to grin!
How neatly spreads his claws,
And welcomes little fishes in,
With gently smiling jaws!

Creative Synthesis

D3

Draw a picture of the crocodile as the poet describes it. Ask your teacher or librarian to help you find books about the Nile River and the crocodiles that live there. How does the description of the crocodile from the poet compare with the pictures and information in your book?

Summarizing

D2

Summarize what is going on in the poem in two sentences or pictures. Be prepared to explain your ideas using information from the poem.

Paraphrasing

D1

Rewrite in your own words what is happening when the poet writes "And welcomes little fishes in/ with gently smiling jaws!"

THE CROCODILE

Name: _____ Date: _____

Playing With Words

F3

Write your own poem with an AB rhyming pattern.

Thinking About Words

F2

Is it important for both stanzas' rhyming patterns to match? Why or why not? What does that mean?

Understanding Words

F1

In a different color, underline the matching rhyming words at the end of each line. For example, if the words *bark* and *hark* rhyme, both words would be underlined with the same color.

THE CROCODILE

Swing Song

by A. A. Milne

Here I go up in my swing
Ever so high.
I am the King of the fields, and the King
Of the town.
I am the King of the earth, and the King
Of the sky.
Here I go up in my swing . . .
Now I go down.

Theme/Concept

C3

This poem is about the concept of power. How is that concept explored in the poem?

Inference

C2

What do you think causes the swinger to be so boastful?

Literary Elements

C1

Poets create patterns of words to produce a pleasing effect. What is the relationship between the direction of the swing and the swinger's identity? Describe the pattern of that relationship.

SWING SONG

Name: _____ **Date:** _____

Creative Synthesis

D3

What do you think about when you swing on the playground? Create a poem that reveals your thoughts.

Summarizing

D2

Summarize the poem in a prose statement and illustrate it.

Paraphrasing

D1

In your own words, describe the scenes the swinger comments on.

SWING SONG

F3

Playing With Words

Create a new title for the poem and
tell why it would be appropriate.

SWING SONG

F2

Thinking About Words

What would the kings of the various areas cited
in the poem do? How are their roles similar and
different, based on their domain? Complete a
chart with their similarities and differences.

F1

Understanding Words

What other words would convey royalty besides
"king" in the poem? What words could be used to
describe a royal person? There is a poetic technique
called *metonymy* that allows a poet to use the
name of an object to represent the person who
it describes. What words could be substituted
for king that would illustrate metonymy?

The Four Friends

by A. A. Milne

Ernest was an elephant, a great big fellow,
Leonard was a lion with a six foot tail,
George was a goat, and his beard was yellow,
And James was a very small snail.

Leonard had a stall, and a great big strong one,
Ernest had a manger, and its walls were thick,
George found a pen, but I think it was the wrong one,
And James sat down on a brick

Ernest started trumpeting, and cracked his manger,
Leonard started roaring, and shivered his stall,
James gave a huffle of a snail in danger
And nobody heard him at all.

Ernest started trumpeting and raised such a rumpus,
Leonard started roaring and trying to kick,
James went on a journey with the goat's new compass
And he reached the end of his brick.

Ernest was an elephant and very well intentioned,
Leonard was a lion with a brave new tail,
George was a goat, as I think I have mentioned,
But James was only a snail.

Generalizations

B3

What generalizations can you make about
Ernest, George, Leonard, and James?
Use your detail chart to decide.

Classifications

B2

How would you categorize the
details given for each animal?

Details

B1

What details does the poet provide about
each animal? Make a chart that names the
animals and describes each detail provided.

THE FOUR FRIENDS

Creative Synthesis

D3

Create a poem that has four animals in it that you describe. Write four lines about each animal. Then conclude the poem in four lines by comparing them to each other.

Summarizing

D2

What can you say about each animal, based on the description provided of each?

Paraphrasing

D1

In your own words, describe what the meaning of the last line is: "But James was only a snail."

THE FOUR FRIENDS

Playing With Words

F3

Give the animals in the poem names
that better describe their characteristics.
Why do your choices work better?

Thinking About Words

F2

How does the poet convey the small size of
James? What are the effects of his being small?

Understanding Words

F1

Look up the word "huffle." Is it a good word
choice for the poem? Why or why not?

THE FOUR FRIENDS

Fire in the Window

by Mary Mapes Dodge

Fire in the window! flashes in the pane!
Fire on the roof-top! blazing weather-vane!
Turn about, weather-vane! put the fire out!
The sun's going down, sir, I haven't a doubt.

FIRE IN THE WINDOW

Theme/Concept

C3

What ideas does the poem convey to you about the power of nature? What power can be seen in rain, wind, and snow? Describe each of these elements in a few words or phrases.

Inference

C2

What do you think the fire in the window is? Why do you think so? What is a weather vane? How could it be a signal for the fire to go out?

Literary Elements

C1

What devices does the poet use to get your attention in the poem?

Creative Synthesis

D3

Create a poem about an ordinary event that occurs every day in the style of this poem. Notice the rhyme scheme, number of lines, and descriptions used.

Summarizing

D2

Summarize the effect the poem has on you.

Paraphrasing

D1

In your own words, describe the purpose of the poem. Why does the author "haven't a doubt" about the sun's going down?

FIRE IN THE WINDOW

Playing With Words

F3

Why does the poet use the first line of the poem as the title? Create a better title for the poem. Why do you think your title is better?

Thinking About Words

F2

What does the sun going down in the poem represent? How would the poem be different if the sun were coming up? Make changes in the poem to show the differences.

Understanding Words

F1

Make a list of words you associate with the sun. Create a description of the sun from your list. How does your description relate to the poem?

FIRE IN THE WINDOW

A Kitten

by Eleanor Farjeon

He's nothing much but fur
And two round eyes of blue,
He has a giant purr
And a midget mew.

He darts and pats the air,
He starts and cocks his ear,
When there is nothing there
For him to see and hear.

He runs around in rings,
But why we cannot tell;
With sideways leaps he springs
At things invisible—

Then half-way through a leap
His startled eyeballs close,
And he drops off to sleep
With one paw on his nose.

A KITTEN

Generalizations

B3

How would you define a kitten? Provide an overall definition, based on your categories.

Classifications

B2

What other kittenish behavior have you observed? (You may select another type of animal if you prefer.) How would you classify or categorize the behaviors?

Details

B1

What are the interesting observations the poet makes about the antics of the kitten? Make a list of the different ones she records.

Creative Synthesis

D3

Create a poem about another animal that describes its defining behaviors. What words are good for describing behavior? Make a list and select the best ones for your own poem. Try to use the rhyming approach seen in this poem.

Summarizing

D2

What is the poem about? Write (or dictate) a short summary of it.

Paraphrasing

D1

In your own words, tell what kitten act is the funniest. Draw a picture to illustrate the behavior.

A KITTEN

Playing With Words

F3

Create a list of rhyming words and put them together at the end of lines you make up in an interesting way. Use the poem as a model for your work.

Thinking About Words

F2

What is the effect of rhyme on how you relate to a poem?

Understanding Words

F1

Identify the pattern of rhyming in this poem. Look at the end of each line and see what the word at the end rhymes with.

A KITTEN

My Shadow

by Robert Louis Stevenson

I have a little shadow that goes in and out with me,
And what can be the use of him is more than I can see.
He is very, very like me from the heels up to the head;
And I see him jump before me, when I jump into my bed.

The funniest thing about him is the way he likes to grow—
Not at all like proper children, which is always very slow;
For he sometimes shoots up taller like an india-rubber ball,
And he sometimes gets so little that
there's none of him at all.

He hasn't got a notion of how children ought to play,
And can only make a fool of me in every sort of way.
He stays so close beside me, he's a coward you can see;
I'd think shame to stick to nursie as
that shadow sticks to me!

One morning, very early, before the sun was up,
I rose and found the shining dew on every buttercup;
But my lazy little shadow, like an arrant sleepy-head,
Had stayed at home behind me and was fast asleep in bed.

MY SHADOW

D3
Creative Synthesis

Select two different ways the author explains shadows in the poem. Model them outside or with a lamp indoors to prove what the author shares.

D2
Summarizing

Explain why the author didn't see the shadow, as described in the last stanza.

D1
Paraphrasing

Retell the following lines in your own words: "For he sometimes shoots up taller like an india-rubber ball/ And he sometimes gets so little that there's none of him at all."

Playing With Words

F3

Select your favorite stanza of the poem and illustrate it. Explain how the author's use of words helped you illustrate your stanza.

Thinking About Words

F2

Why is the use of personification important in the poem? How would the poem be different if the author just told about shadows without giving them human qualities?

Understanding Words

F1

Personification is when the author gives something that isn't real person-like qualities. How does the poet use personification to make the shadow seem like a real person?

MY SHADOW

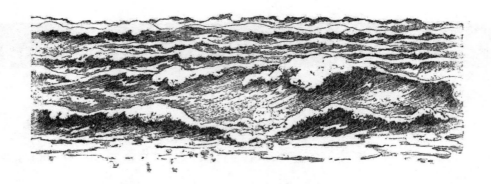

Little Things

by Ebenezer Cobham Brewer

Little drops of water,
Little grains of sand,
Make the mighty ocean
And the pleasant land.

Thus the little minutes,
Humble though they be,
Make the mighty ages
Of eternity.

Theme/Concept

C3

What is the message of this poem?
How do you know?

Inference

C2

What does the author mean by "Thus the little minutes,/ Humble though they be,/ Make the mighty ages/ Of eternity"?

Literary Elements

C1

Make a list of the words in the poem that you don't know and then look up their definitions. Write a synonym or draw a picture to represent the new words.

LITTLE THINGS

Playing With Words

F3

The author uses the relationship between drops of water and the oceans as well as minutes and eternity. Write or draw at least three other relationships you can think of from your own experience, and then tell how your ideas show the same relationships as the words in the poem.

Thinking About Words

F2

Draw a picture to represent each sentence of the poem. Be prepared to explain it.

Understanding Words

F1

Underline the most important words in the poem. Why are those words important?

LITTLE THINGS

Mummy Slept Late and Daddy Fixed Breakfast

by John Ciardi

Daddy fixed the breakfast.
He made us each a waffle.
It looked like gravel pudding.
It tasted something awful.

"Ha, ha," he said, "I'll try again.
This time I'll get it right."
But what I got was in between
Bituminous and anthracite.*

"A little too well done? Oh well,
I'll have to start all over."
That time what landed on my plate
Looked like a manhole cover.

I tried to cut it with a fork:
The fork gave off a spark.
I tried a knife and twisted it
Into a question mark.

Continues
*Types of coal

I tried it with a hack-saw.
I tried it with a torch.
It didn't even make a dent.
It didn't even scorch.

The next time Dad gets breakfast
When Mummy's sleeping late,
I think I'll skip the waffles.
I'd rather eat the plate.

 Jacob's Ladder Reading Comprehension Program Primary 1 © Prufrock Press • This page may be photocopied or reproduced with permission for single classroom use.

Consequences and Implications

A3

What are the consequences of
Dad's poor cooking skills?

Cause and Effect

A2

The author tells many causes and effects.
For example, he tried to cut the waffle,
and it bent the fork. Create a chart of
other cause-and-effect relationships in the
poem. Write them in your own words.

Sequencing

A1

Draw a comic strip to outline the sequence of
events in the story. Use at least four pictures.

MUMMY SLEPT LATE AND DADDY FIXED BREAKFAST

Playing With Words

F3

Think of something that happened to you that is either really good or really unpleasant. Write a phrase or sentence using hyperbole to exaggerate your experience. Illustrate it.

Thinking About Words

F2

How does the use of hyperbole make the poem funny?

Understanding Words

F1

The author uses hyperbole (exaggeration) to make the poem funny. Find at least four exaggerations used in the poem and underline them. Draw a picture of the one you think is the funniest.

MUMMY SLEPT LATE AND DADDY FIXED BREAKFAST

Whether the Weather

by Anonymous

Whether the weather be fine
Or whether the weather be not
Whether the weather be cold
Or whether the weather be hot,
We'll weather the weather
Whatever the weather,
Whether we like it or not!

Creative Synthesis

D3

Use the words *weather*, *weather*, and *whether* (or another word set of your choice) to write a tongue-twister that makes sense for your friends.

Summarizing

D2

Explain in your own words and no more than one sentence what the poem is about.

Paraphrasing

D1

In your own words, explain the following phrase "We'll weather the weather." How are the two words different even though they are spelled the same?

WHETHER THE WEATHER

WHETHER THE WEATHER

Playing With Words

F3

Select one of your word pairs from the second rung, and write a poem using the words in as many ways as possible.

Thinking About Words

F2

Make a list of at least 5 additional word pairs that sound the same but are spelled differently. Here's an example: see, sea.

Understanding Words

F1

What is the difference between the words *whether* and *weather*? Define both of them and provide an example of each.

Pre- and Postassessments, Rubric, and Discussion Checklist

Appendix A contains the pre- and postassessment readings and questions, as well as a rubric for scoring the assessments. The preassessment should be administered before any work with *Jacob's Ladder* is conducted. After all of the readings and ladders have been completed, the postassessment can be given to track student improvement on the ladder skill sets.

Appendix A also includes a discussion checklist that teachers may use to analyze whether or not students understand key content through group or individual responses that may not be in writing.

Pretest: Aesop's Fables

Please read (or listen) to the following fable and write (or dictate) responses to the following questions.

The Crow and the Serpent
Originally told by Aesop

A Crow in great want of food saw a Serpent asleep in a sunny nook, and flying down, greedily seized him. The Serpent, turning about, bit the Crow with a mortal wound. In the agony of death, the bird exclaimed: "O unhappy me! who have found in that which I deemed a happy windfall the source of my destruction."

1. Summarize the fable in your own words.

_____

_____

_____

_____

_____

_____

2. What did the Crow do to bring about his own destruction? How could he have prevented it?

_____

_____

_____

_____

3. How did the story make you feel? What lesson did you learn from it?

_____

_____

_____

_____

Posttest: Aesop's Fables

Please read (or listen) to the following fable and write (or dictate) responses to the following questions.

The Peacock and Juno
Originally told by Aesop

The Peacock made complaint to Juno that, while the nightingale pleased every ear with his song, he himself no sooner opened his mouth than he became a laughingstock to all who heard him. The Goddess, to console him, said, "But you far excel in beauty and in size. The splendor of the emerald shines in your neck and you unfold a tail gorgeous with painted plumage." "But for what purpose have I," said the bird, "this dumb beauty so long as I am surpassed in song?' "The lot of each," replied Juno, "has been assigned by the will of the Fates—to thee, beauty; to the eagle, strength; to the nightingale, song; to the raven, favorable, and to the crow, unfavorable auguries. These are all contented with the endowments allotted to them."

Name: _____ Date: _____

1. Summarize the fable in your own words.

_____

_____

_____

_____

2. What is Juno's argument to the Peacock as to why he should feel content?

_____

_____

_____

_____

3. What lesson do you think the fable is trying to convey?

_____

_____

_____

_____

Rubric for Scoring Aesop's Fables

4 = Highly Effective   3= Effective   2 = Somewhat Effective   1 = Not Effective

Summary of Fable	4	3	2	1
Students who are highly effective will outline the key points of the summary with supporting and accurate evidence from the text in a clear and concise format.				

Explanation of Fable or Moral	4	3	2	1
Students who are highly effective will accurately and articulately explain the fable or moral, citing evidence from the story and explaining the figurative meaning of the fable instead of the literal interpretation.				

Impact on the Reader/Application to Life	4	3	2	1
Students who are highly effective will make connections to life while referring back to the story's plot or meaning as a guide for discussion and decision. Students will stay on task with the story theme as part of the explanation and explain clear linkages between the text and the reader.				

Teacher Notes and Evidence of Student's Effectiveness:

Name: _____ Date: _____

Discussion Checklist:
A Guide for Monitoring Student Talk

1 = rarely　　　**2 = sometimes**　　　**3 = most of the time**

The student:	1	2	3
a. Provides evidence from the text to support ideas without being prompted.			
b. Contributes to discussions by asking questions of other students.			
c. Explains the figurative interpretation of a text instead of the literal one.			
d. Waits his or her turn for talking without interrupting others.			
e. Comes prepared to discuss ideas in a group.			
f. Is respectful of all group members' ideas.			
g. Asks other students for evidence in a story before making a judgment.			
h. Uses discussion prompts to promote instead of stifle conversation.			
i. Clearly articulates ideas in an understandable way.			
j. Is willing to change his or her mind if given acceptable evidence.			
Teacher Evidence of Student Progress:			

Classroom Diagnostic Forms

Appendix B contains classroom diagnostic forms. These forms are for teachers and are designed to aid them in keeping track of the progress and skill mastery of their students. With these charts, teachers can record student progress in relation to each ladder skill within a genre and select additional ladders and readings based on student needs.

Classroom Diagnostic Form

Short Stories

Use this document to record student completion of ladder sets with the assessment of work.

0 = Needs More Practice With the Given Skill Set   1 = Understands and Applies Skills   2 = Applies Skills Very Effectively

Student Name	Ella Sarah Gets Dressed			Flotsam			The Red Book			Kitten's First Full Moon			A Sick Day for Amos McGee			The Hare and the Tortoise			Owen			Anno's Journey			Doctor De Soto			Come Away From the Water, Shirley		
	A	E		A	C	D	A	C	D	C	E	F	A	C	D	B	C	F	A	C	E	A	B	D	A	C	D	B	C	D

Jacob's Ladder Reading Comprehension Program Primary 1 © Prufrock Press • This page may be photocopied or reproduced with permission for single classroom use.

Classroom Diagnostic Form

Short Stories

Use this document to record student completion of ladder sets with the assessment of work.

0 = Needs More Practice With the Given Skill Set   1 = Understands and Applies Skills   2 = Applies Skills Very Effectively

Student Name	Noah's Ark				There's a Nightmare in My Closet				Ox-Cart Man				The Man Who Walked Between the Towers				Paul Bunyan				The Girl Who Loved Wild Horses				Make Way for Ducklings				The Polar Express				The Ants and the Grasshopper				Where the Wild Things Are			
	A	C	D		B	D			A	C	F		A	B	E		B	C	D		A	C	D		A	B	D		A	B	C		A	C		C		B	D	E

Classroom Diagnostic Form
Poetry

Use this document to record student completion of ladder sets with the assessment of work.

0 = Needs More Practice With the Given Skill Set   1 = Understands and Applies Skills   2 = Applies Skills Very Effectively

Student Name	"Daffodowndilly"			"The Crocodile"		"Swing Song"			"The Four Friends"			"Fire in the Window"			"A Kitten"			"My Shadow"		"Little Things"		"Mummy Slept Late and Daddy Fixed Breakfast"		"Whether the Weather"	
	A	C	F	D	F	C	D	F	B	D	F	C	D	F	B	D	F	D	F	C	F	A	F	D	F

About the Authors

Tamra Stambaugh is a research assistant professor of special education and director of Programs for Talented Youth (PTY) at Vanderbilt University. She holds a Ph.D. in education policy, planning, and leadership with an emphasis on gifted education and instructional supervision. Since 1991, she has taught gifted students of varying grade levels, evaluated district gifted programs around the country, trained countless educators in research-based best practices for gifted students, and contributed significant findings to the field of gifted education and talent development as principal and co-principal investigator or manager of a variety of research grants. She is the co-author of *Comprehensive Curriculum for Gifted Learners* (with Joyce VanTassel-Baska) and *Effective Curriculum for Underserved Gifted Students* (with Kimberley Chandler). Stambaugh has also authored or coauthored journal articles and book chapters on a variety of topics focusing on curriculum, instruction, teacher change, and leadership.

In her role as director of Vanderbilt PTY, she directs day and residential talent development programs for gifted students in grades kindergarten through high school. She also designs and leads research projects, provides professional development opportunities for teachers, and consults about gifted education with educators, parents, and community members.

Joyce L. VanTassel-Baska is Professor Emerita at The College of William and Mary, where she founded the Center for Gifted Education. Formerly she initiated and directed the Center for Talent Development at Northwestern University. Joyce has also served as state director of gifted programs in

Illinois, a regional director, a local coordinator of gifted programs, and a teacher of gifted high school students. Her major research interests are in the talent development process and effective curricular interventions with the gifted.

She is the author of 22 books and has written more than 500 other publications on gifted education. She was the editor of *Gifted and Talented International* for several years and received the Distinguished Scholar Award in 1997 from the National Association for Gifted Children and the Outstanding Faculty Award from the State Council of Higher Education in Virginia in 1993. She received the Distinguished Alumna Achievement Award from the University of Toledo in 2003, the President's Award from the World Council on Gifted and Talented in 2005, and the Collaboration and Diversity Service Award from CEC-TAG in 2007.